For my fairy godchildren:
Leila, Zuri and Cassius
E. R.

To my family and friends.
Thank you for being there.
A. S.

And Everything Will Be Glad to See You gathers poems from all over the world.
Regional spellings and usage have been retained in order to preserve the integrity of the originals.

First published 2022 by Nosy Crow Ltd
The Crow's Nest, 14 Baden Place, Crosby Row, London, SE1 1YW, UK
Nosy Crow Eireann Ltd, 44 Orchard Grove, Kenmare, Co Kerry, V93 FY22, Ireland
www.nosycrow.com

ISBN 978 1 78800 921 8

The acknowledgements on pages 140-141 constitute an extension of this copyright page.

A CIP catalogue record for this book is available from the British Library.

Printed in China.
Papers used by Nosy Crow are made from wood grown in sustainable forests.

MIX
Paper from responsible sources
FSC® C104723

10 9 8 7 6 5 4 3 2 1

And Everything Will Be Glad to See You

Poems by Women and Girls

Selected by
Ella Risbridger

Illustrated by
Anna Shepeta

INTRODUCTION

When I was small, my great-grandmother gave me a poetry book. Her name was Granny M and Granny M had tins of marbles in her cupboard and interesting books that smelled of time. She used to let us drive her mobility scooter round her cul-de-sac. The mobility scooter was called Matilda. I loved her – my granny, not the scooter – very much.

Anyway, when I was very small, she gave me a poetry book. It was a collection of poems from all sorts of poets and all sorts of places: an anthology. Granny M loved poems, and she wanted me to love them too. Luckily, I did.

When you read a poem, you see, you get to see the world like someone else sees it. You get to see what they see and feel what they feel. You get to think, "Oh my gosh, ME TOO", or "I NEVER THOUGHT OF IT LIKE THAT BEFORE", and both of those feelings are magic. Sometimes I think those are the feelings that make us human: the feelings that make us know what it's like to be one person alive in a world full of other people. I love those feelings, and I knew when I first read that poetry book that I would never, ever, ever get tired of them.

There is a picture of me somewhere as that very small person, sitting on the stairs with my legs dangling, reading that book; and I remember exactly what I was thinking, sitting there. I was thinking, "One day, I am going to grow up and make books just like this one." So that is what I have done, more or less.

I say "more or less", because this book isn't exactly like that one my granny gave me so long ago. You'll find some of the same poems in this one, because I loved them – but this book is different. It's different because, in this book, we've left out all the poems by boys and men.

Now, please don't put the book back on the shelf right away. This might seem really unfair, but give me a minute, and I will try to explain why.

Most of the poems in this book are by women.

Some of the poems in this book are by girls. (Some of those girls are as young as six or seven years old!)

At least one of the poems in this book is by a non-binary person. ("Non-binary person" is a quick way of describing a person who isn't actually a boy or a girl. When you're making a collection of poems sorted by gender, it can be tricky to figure out where to put poems by non-binary people. This means they often get left out of collections by boys and left out of collections by girls. Some non-binary people would like to be in both kinds of collection, and some would like to be in one kind over the other, and some in neither – so you have to ask every time. Luckily for us, we've been able to include a poem by a brilliant non-binary writer in this book! We really loved the poem, and when we talked to the writer about it, they said they would really love to be included. I wonder if you can spot it?)

So, we've got poems by women, and girls, and non-binary people – and we've also got poems by someone named Anonymous.

Anonymous, as you probably already know, means that we don't know who wrote it: we don't know anything about them. We don't know their name, or who they were, or where they came from – and I have put in some poems by Anonymous because often in history what "Anonymous" really means is that the writer was a woman.

"I would venture to guess," wrote Virginia Woolf once, "that Anon, who wrote so many poems without signing them, was often a woman." (Virginia Woolf was a famous author, and she said many smart things about writing, and about women.)

But you are probably wondering why this would be, and actually, why it would matter to me at all that the writer is a woman. You might even be wondering whether it's really fair to have a collection of poems that are only by women and girls. Doesn't that leave other people out? What about boys and men?

These are all good questions and to answer them properly we have to look at the big picture. We have to look at the whole way our world is organised, and the whole history of the way we write things, and the whole history of who gets to write things.

Another very famous writer, Elizabeth Bishop, asked these questions too. She thought it was so obviously a bad idea that she refused to let anyone put her poems into an anthology like this at all. (We did ask anyway, though, because her poems are so good.)

Elizabeth Bishop thought that separating art out into art-by-men and art-by-women made it seem like art-by-men and art-by-women were completely different – like all boys' art had something in common that it didn't share with girls' art, and the same the other way round. Elizabeth Bishop thought that making anthologies just full of writing by men or just full of writing by women made it seem like the art that boys make is fundamentally different from the art that girls make. For example, if all the children in a class wrote poems, would you be able to tell which ones were written by girls if you didn't look at the names? Would you be able to say that all girls wrote poems like this, or all boys wrote poems like that? If you couldn't, then what's the point of making an anthology where the only thing the poets have in common is what's under their clothes? That's what Elizabeth Bishop thought, anyway, and maybe you agree with her.

Sometimes I think that I do, but then I think about this: in that first poetry book my granny gave me, there were many more poems by men than there were by women. Actually, this is the case in most poetry anthologies. Sometimes you have to turn twenty or thirty or even forty pages to find a poem that isn't written by a man. And when they make lists of famous poets in history, they are almost always men. And when they ask people to name famous poets, they almost always say men. And all but one of the UK's Poets Laureate – a special job, and some say the highest honour for poets – have been men. Twenty men![1] One woman!

Isn't that ridiculous? But it's true, all the same. So why would this ridiculous thing be true? Well, here's something unfair: male poets tend to be more famous than female poets, because they always have been. I know!

Books tend to be full of poems by boys and men because they have always been the ones who got to publish their poems in books. This is what we call "structural bias", which is a fancy way of saying that the problems are built into the structure of our world, i.e. the way our world works.

Because women haven't always been allowed the space to think, and the peace and quiet to make those thoughts into something beautiful. Women haven't always been allowed to explain why what they saw and what they thought mattered just as much as the things men saw and thought. Women couldn't vote, so they couldn't change anything. Most women couldn't even control their own property or decide what happened to their own children. Some couldn't even choose who they married, or how they spent their lives at all. Women were not supposed to have a voice. Don't ask me why. It doesn't make sense to me, either. But that was the way it was, for a very long time.

For a long time, people who seemed like girls and women didn't get taken seriously as poets, or – often – as people.

That includes people who were sorted into the "girl" category at birth, and never felt like it fitted them. It includes people who were sorted into the "boy" box at birth and never felt like that fitted them. It includes boys and men who act in "girly" ways. It includes anyone, basically, who doesn't fit into an old-fashioned idea of what a "man" should be – and this is also part of that "structural bias" thing I said about earlier. People who are girls, or who are sorted into the girl category at birth, or do "girly" things, have been taken less seriously for hundreds of years. And that's one reason we wanted to make this book.

---

[1] In America it's actually a bit better, but not much – six women, and sixteen men. This is mostly for complicated reasons to do with the slightly different definitions of Poet Laureate; in America you get one year, but in the UK you do it for life or ten years. I don't know why this is.

But there have always been some women who made it, I promise. You'll find lots of them in this book. There have always been some brave and lucky and clever ones who wrote, no matter how much the world didn't want them to do it; and sometimes they used their own name and just hoped people would take them seriously; and sometimes they used a more masculine-sounding name; and sometimes they used no name at all.

And all of this, I hope, goes some way to explaining why all the poems in this book except one are by women and girls. It isn't that art by boys is different from art by girls. It's just that, all through history, we've simply paid it lots more attention. And that's not fair, either.

This book is my best shot at being fair. This book is my best shot at showing you all the brave, lucky, clever girls and women who wrote poems when nobody really wanted them to. This book is my best shot at making sure that whenever someone picks up a poetry book, they'll find plenty of poems by girls, my best shot at making sure that when someone asks you to think of a poet, you think of a woman just as quickly as you think of a man. This is a world that belongs to everyone – to women and men and everyone in between – and everyone should get a chance to show you the world the way they see it.

And one day, maybe you'll see something, and want to tell the world about it, and you'll maybe write it down in a poem of your own. And maybe I'll see it, and think, "Oh my gosh, ME TOO", or maybe I'll think, "I NEVER THOUGHT OF IT LIKE THAT BEFORE", and both those things will be brilliant feelings. Maybe someone else will see it. Maybe the whole world will see it. Maybe one day you'll even put it in a poetry anthology, more or less like this one.

I say "more or less", of course, because your anthology will be different. You'll take poems from all the different books you love, and all the different books you write. You'll put in it all the poems that have made "your one wild and precious life", which is a line from a poem in this book. And then, maybe, you'll give it to someone, and you'll be part of a whole beautiful web of reading things, and loving things, and brave and lucky and clever people trying to show the world the things that matter to them, and doing it whether or not anyone told them they could.

And maybe you won't do any of these things. Maybe you'll just remember that someone loved you enough to give you this book, and that will be enough. Whatever you do, I want you to be brave, and I want you to be lucky. I want you to be free to show the world what you want from it – I want you to see it and be glad, and I want everything to be glad to see you right back. That's why we chose the title we chose for this book, which is another line from a poem. Poems can give you a life where you see things differently, and you're glad about it, and then everything will be glad to see you, too.

Love, always,

Ella

x

Ella Risbridger

93 PERCENT STARDUST

We have calcium in our bones,
iron in our veins,
carbon in our souls,
and nitrogen in our brains.
93 percent stardust,
with souls made of flames,
we are all just stars
that have people names.

Nikita Gill

COMET

(To be read as quickly as possible, in as few breaths as you can manage.)

I'm a spinning, winning, tripping, zipping, super-sonic ice queen:
see my moon zoom, clock my rocket, watch me splutter tricksy space-steam.

I'm the dust bomb, I'm the freeze sneeze, I'm the top galactic jockey
made (they think) of gas and ice and mystery bits of something rocky.

Oh I sting a sherbet orbit, running rings round star or planet;
should I shoot too near the sun, my tail hots up: *ouch* – OUCH – *please fan it!*

And I'm told I hold the answer to the galaxy's top question:
that my middle's made of history (no surprise I've indigestion)

but for now I sprint and skid and whisk and bolt and belt and bomb it;
I'm that hell-for-leather, lunging, plunging, helter-skelter COMET.

Kate Wakeling

WHAT IS NOW WILL SOON BE PAST

Just because you do it
doesn't mean you always will.
Whether you're dancing dust
or breathing light
you're never exactly the same,
twice.

Yrsa Daley-Ward

I SAW

I saw a peacock with a fiery tail
I saw a blazing comet drop down hail
I saw a cloud with ivy circled round
I saw a sturdy oak creep on the ground
I saw an ant swallow up a whale
I saw a raging sea brim full of ale
I saw a Venice glass sixteen foot deep
I saw a well full of men's tears that weep
I saw their eyes all in a flame of fire
I saw a house as big as the moon and higher
I saw the sun even in the midst of night
I saw the man that saw this wondrous sight.

Anonymous

THIS RAY

This ray of sun I claim,
When warmth begins to wane.
On days when darkness lingers
In cold and ghastly winters,
I'll recall its intensity
that day it shined on me.

Triska Hamid

STARS AND DANDELIONS

Deep in the blue sky,
like pebbles at the bottom of the sea,
lie the stars unseen in daylight
until night comes.
    You can't see them, but they are there.
    Unseen things are still there.

The withered, seedless dandelions
hidden in the cracks of the roof tile
wait silently for spring,
their strong roots unseen.
    You can't see them, but they are there.
    Unseen things are still there.

Misuzu Kaneko

GHAZAL WITH RAIN AND BIRDS

Day opens its eyes: sky's pillowed with cloud.
Each morning's a gift, a melody bright with birds.

Rain is beginning, and rain is ending,
longed-for and sudden, as heavy, as light as birds.

A tree is a village, a garden, a town,
a thunder of wingbeats, a day and a night of birds.

Streets freshly watered, a telephone line
is strung as if pearled, with white after white after white bird.

The breeze brings a kite painted with flowers –
it's caught in the arms of the tree, alight with birds.

Come to the river, to its bed full of stones,
Come rest on the green of its bank, a delight for birds.

Shazea Quraishi

SING A SONG OF PEOPLE

Sing a song of people
Walking fast or slow;
People in the city
Up and down they go.

People on the sidewalk,
People on the bus;
People passing, passing,
In back and front of us.
People on the subway
Underneath the ground;
People riding taxis
Round and round and round.

People with their hats on,
Going in the doors;
People with umbrellas
When it rains and pours.
People in tall buildings
And in stores below;
Riding elevators
Up and down they go.

People walking singly,
People in a crowd;
People saying nothing,
People talking loud.
People laughing, smiling,
Grumpy people too;
People who just hurry
And never look at you!

Sing a song of people
Who like to come and go;
Sing of city people
You see but never know!

Lois Lenski

PEOPLE ARE A LIVING STRUCTURE LIKE A CORAL REEF

People love to clean their ears and I love people
very much They are everywhere! Every single
thing I love I love for windows only and if
one window reflects another then friends
for me it's all over And in the windows are trees
and in the windows are people What are they even doing
with their hunger and in their new shirts They are
taking care of themselves and they are taking each other out
for lunch Oh even the rain has to love them People
are just too attractive! and the rain places itself
on the window in order to be closer to the people
the ones who are eating The ones who are
busting out vigor Oh people You have to love
people They are so much like ourselves

Heather Christle

TO OUR DAUGHTER

And she is beautiful, our daughter.
Only six months, but a person.
She turns to look at everything, out walking.
All so precious. I mustn't disturb it with words.
People are like great clowns,
Blossom like balloons, black pigeons like eagles,
Water beyond belief.

She holds out her hand to air,
Sea, sky, wind, sun, movement, stillness,
And wants to hold them all.
My finger is her earth connection, me, and earth.

Her head is like an apple, or an egg.
Skin stretched fine over a strong casing,
Her whole being developing from within.
And from without: the answer.

And she sings, long notes from the belly or the throat,
Her legs kick her feet up to her nose,
She rests—laid still like a large rose.
She is our child,
The world is not hers, she has to win it.

Jennifer Armitage

NINA'S SONG

Nina, come to Scotland
Nina come soon
We'll show you the wee-est field mouse
And the biggest, roundest moon.

The million-zillion stars'll *amaze* you –
So bright and so far . . .
Pick one and we'll sing you
Twinkle, twinkle little star

Come soon, Nina,
Come and never wonder why
There can be three perfect rainbows
In just one wide sky –

Just enjoy the bonny colours
Nina, never mind their names –
Although it's true
We will very much enjoy teaching you
Your *red, orange, yellow, green and blue*
Your *violet* and *indigo,*
And every colour that we know
Wee Nina, all the same.

And everything will be glad to see you
All the singing birds will go,
Nice to meet you, new wee Nina,
Hey, Nina – hello!

Liz Lochhead

WHERE DID THE BABY GO?

I cannot remember –
And neither can my mother –
Just when it was our baby
Turned into my brother.

Julie Holder

SEVEN SISTERS

Seven sisters standing
shoulder to chalky shoulder –
Seven sisters huddling to Sussex mist
open-armed to sun's expansive kiss
yet straight and firm as Victorian maidens
all kin to Dover – the green-shawled
grandmother of all cliffs.

Grace Nichols

I HAD FOUR BROTHERS

I had four brothers over the sea,
And they each sent a present to me.

The first sent a goose without any bone,
The second sent a cherry without any stone.

The third sent a blanket without any thread,
The fourth sent a book that could not be read.

How could there be a goose without any bone?
How could there be a cherry without any stone?

How could there be a blanket without any thread?
How could there be a book that could not be read?

Anonymous

COROMANDEL FISHERS

EXTRACT

Rise, brothers, rise, the wakening skies
pray to the morning light.
The wind lies asleep in the arms of the dawn
like a child that has cried all night.
Come, let us gather our nets from the shore,
and set our *catamarans* free,
To capture the leaping wealth of the tide,
for we are the sons of the sea.

No longer delay, let us hasten away
in the track of the seagull's call,
The sea is our mother, the cloud is our brother,
the waves are our comrades all.
What though we toss at the fall of the sun
where the hand of the sea-god drives?
He who holds the storm by the hair,
will hide in his breast our lives.

Sarojini Naidu

BATH TIME
FOR MY SISTER

I had two years on you,
adrift
in a great wet wash.

I slapped
against the taps,
got lost hunting
big fish soap,

soaked walls
with slipping under.
Just me in a small ship

all at sea.

So I call your little arms
compass,
give your tiny legs
the title *map*.

You delineated land,
steered true;

you understood
north, south,
sunrise
and occasional flags.

You helped me
unknot the stars

and navigate
to larger arms,
shore.

Rachel Piercey

GRANNY GRANNY
PLEASE COMB MY HAIR

Granny Granny
please comb my hair
you always take your time
you always take such care

You put me to sit on a cushion
between your knees
you rub a little coconut oil
parting gentle as a breeze

Mummy Mummy
she's always in a hurry – hurry
rush
she pulls my hair
sometimes she tugs

But Granny
you have all the time in the world
and when you're finished
you always turn my head and say
"Now who's a nice girl."

Grace Nichols

GETTING READY FOR SCHOOL

Kate, Kate,
I know you'll be late!
Here is your satchel and here is your slate.
Don't go like that, Child, your hair's in a state –
Kate! Kate! Kate!

Kate, Kate,
It's twenty to nine,
Take your umbrella, it may not be fine.
Oh, what a hanky – you'd better take mine –
Kate! Kate! Kate!

Kate, Kate,
You haven't your fare!
Here are your sandwiches on the hall chair.
What's that? – your hockey stick – where darling where?
Kate! Kate! Kate!

Kate, Kate,
Your gym shoes are here,
Won't you be needing your pencil-box, dear?
Try to speak slower, love, Mother can't hear –
Kate! Kate! Kate!

Kate, Kate,
You'd better not wait,
The two little Smith girls have just passed the gate.
Hurry up, darling, I know you'll be late –
Kate! Kate! Kate!

Caryl Brahms

MRS HAMILTON'S REGISTER

Grace and beauty?
Annie, here.
Eternal blossom?
Amarachi, here.
Celestial spirit?
Devashree, here.
One to admire?
Emily, here.
Light of a girl?
Ella, here.
Heaven's benevolence?
Gianina, here.
Hill near meadows?
Georgina, here.
Kind angel?
Juanaya, here.
Sea of riches?
Molly, here.
Victorious heart?
Nicola, here.
Little one?
Polly, here.
Lovely flower?
Rosie, here.
Twilight hour?
Sharvari, here.
Soft dark eyes?
Siya, here.
Thank you, girls.
Thank you, Mrs Hamilton.

Carol Ann Duffy

SALLY

She was a dog-rose kind of girl:
elusive, scattery as petals;
scratchy sometimes, tripping you like briars.
She teased the boys
turning this way and that, not to be tamed
or taught any more than the wind.
Even in school the word "ought"
had no meaning for Sally.
On dull days
she'd sit quiet as a mole at her desk
delving in thought.
But when the sun called
she was gone, running the blue day down
till the warm hedgerows prickled the dusk
and moths flickered out.

Her mother scolded; Dad
gave her the hazel-switch,
said her head was stuffed with feathers
and a starling tongue.
But they couldn't take the shine out of her.
Even when it rained
you felt the sun saved under her skin.
She'd a way of escape
laughing at you from the bright end of a tunnel,
leaving you in the dark.

Phoebe Hesketh

BRENDON GALLACHER

FOR MY BROTHER, MAXIE

He was seven and I was six, my Brendon Gallacher.
He was Irish and I was Scottish, my Brendon Gallacher.
His father was in prison; he was a cat burglar.
My father was a communist party full-time worker.
He had six brothers and I had one, my Brendon Gallacher.

He would hold my hand and take me by the river
Where we'd talk all about his family being poor.
He'd get his mum out of Glasgow when he got older.
A wee holiday some place nice. Some place far.
I'd tell my mum about my Brendon Gallacher.

How his mum drank and his daddy was a cat burglar.
And she'd say, "Why not have him round to dinner?"
No, no, I'd say, he's got big holes in his trousers.
I like meeting him by the burn in the open air.
Then one day after we'd been friends two years,

One day when it was pouring and I was indoors,
My mum says to me, "I was talking to Mrs Moir
Who lives next door to your Brendon Gallacher
Didn't you say his address was 24 Novar?
She says there are no Gallachers at 24 Novar

There never have been any Gallachers next door."
And he died then, my Brendon Gallacher,
Flat out on my bedroom floor, his spiky hair,
His impish grin, his funny flapping ear.
Oh Brendon, oh my Brendon Gallacher.

Jackie Kay

THE HILL WE CLIMB

EXTRACT

The new dawn blooms as we free it,
For there is always light,
If only we're brave enough to see it,
If only we're brave enough to be it.

Amanda Gorman

THERE IS A POEM

scratched onto the walls of my throat
no one has heard it
but it is there

Kai Cheng Thom

JOURNEY'S END

I turn the final page
of the final book,
swallowing each word
of wisdom.
I breathe deep
and feel
something soft but strong
brushing once knobby
shoulder blades,
a quiet unfolding of feathery limbs
emerging from bone and skin.
I thank Miss Mae,
Miss Angelina, Miss Anne,
and all the others
for these new and mighty
glistening things
called wings.
They lift me
from the smallness
of others'
expectations,
reminding me
that I am more
than anyone
gives me credit for.

Nikki Grimes

AUNTIE LUCILLE

AFTER LUCILLE CLIFTON

Auntie Lucille was born with
six fingers on each hand.
This, she wrote, went back through all
the women in her bloodline, all the way
across the sea, to Dahomey – a place
which isn't called that any more.

Not that I've ever been there,
or known Lucille myself.
She's not my mum's sister, not even
Mum's friend – just Auntie Lucille
who smiles from the cover of her book,
a patron saint of black girls anywhere,
a healer of history with soft words.

Any poet's pen is heavy, some say
it takes two hands to hold one.
Weighed down by countless stories,
it's a wonder that a writer writes at all, when
words fail or escape, facts become myths,
or worse, forgotten. Still, if anyone could tell
how to carry the past in one piece, Auntie Lucille,
with twelve fingers, would know.

Victoria Adukwei Bulley

A NEW POET

Finding a new poet
is like finding a new wildflower
out in the woods. You don't see

its name in the flower books, and
nobody you tell believes
in its odd color or the way

its leaves grow in splayed rows
down the whole length of the page. In fact
the very page smells of spilled

red wine and the mustiness of the sea
on a foggy day – the odor of truth
and of lying.

And the words are so familiar,
so strangely new, words
you almost wrote yourself, if only

in your dream there had been a pencil
or a pen or even a paintbrush,
if only there had been a flower.

Linda Pastan

THIS IS A POEM

This is a poem about god looks after things:
He looks after lions, mooses and reindeer and tigers,
Anything that dies,
and mans and little girls when they get to be old,
and mothers he can look after,
and god can look after many old things.
That's why I do this.

Hilary-Anne Farley, age 5

GOD

The moon is a silver hubcap
up in the sky.
It is on God's unicycle.
He rides up high.

On the motorway in the black sky
the stars are streetlights
for God
to show him where to fly.

The planets are traffic lights.
Mars is a red stoplight.
At Saturn he has to wait.
When he gets to Jupiter
he has to go

The clouds are God's thought balloons
sailing by.
He thinks about what we're doing.
He knows I am writing a poem now.

Laura Ranger, age 6

HOW TO EAT A POEM

Don't be polite.
Bite in.
Pick it up with your fingers and lick the juice that

may run down your chin.
It is ready and ripe now, whenever you are.
You do not need a knife or fork or spoon
or plate or napkin or tablecloth.

For there is no core
or stem
or rind
or pit
or seed
or skin
to throw away.

Eve Merriam

GOBLIN MARKET

EXTRACT

Morning and evening
Maids heard the goblins cry:
"Come buy our orchard fruits,
Come buy, come buy:
Apples and quinces,
Lemons and oranges,
Plump unpecked cherries,
Melons and raspberries,
Bloom-down-cheeked peaches.
Swart-headed mulberries,
Wild free-born cranberries,
Crab-apples, dewberries,
Pine-apples, blackberries,
Apricots, strawberries; –
All ripe together
In summer weather –
Morns that pass by,
Fair eves that fly;
Come buy, come buy:
Our grapes fresh from the vine,
Pomegranates full and fine,
Dates and sharp bullaces,
Rare peaches and greengages,
Damsons and bilberries,
Taste them and try:
Currants and gooseberries,
Bright fire-like barberries,
Figs to fill your mouth,
Citrons from the South,
Sweet to tongue and sound to eye;
Come buy, come buy."

Christina Rossetti

KENSINGTON MARKET

Colours
Colours
Colours everywhere
colours of food
    and
colours of people
music sounding
music pounding
Kensington Market on a
    Saturday morning.

Every Saturday morning
Mom takes her shopping basket
and we go to Kensington Market
Bananas
yams
pumpkin
mangos
okras
and
"whappen"!
Caribbean scent.

Fish with sad eyes
eels
salmon
snapper
and the pretty parrot
Portuguese/Atlantic
Nuts and dried fruits
Mexican herbs and spices
it's Pacos' store
and "Como estas".

Chop suey
fried rice
spices from the east
it's Chinese.

The smell of cloves
drifts down the street
it's coming from
the Indonesian restaurant.

All of these mix with music
the sound of
Soca jamming
and
Reggae blasting
"yeah man"!

Colours of food
colours of people
colours of scents
colours of sounds
RED GREEN AND GOLD
Kensington Market on a
    Saturday morning.

Afua Cooper

THE ORANGE

At lunchtime I bought a huge orange –
The size of it made us all laugh.
I peeled it and shared it with Robert and Dave –
They got quarters and I had a half.

And that orange, it made me so happy,
As ordinary things often do
Just lately. The shopping. A walk in the park.
This is peace and contentment. It's new.

The rest of the day was quite easy.
I did all the jobs on my list
And enjoyed them and had some time over.
I love you. I'm glad I exist.

Wendy Cope

WHAT IS PINK?

What is pink? A rose is pink
By the fountain's brink.
What is red? A poppy's red
In its barley bed.
What is blue? The sky is blue
Where the clouds float through.
What is white? A swan is white
Sailing in the light.
What is yellow? Pears are yellow,
Rich and ripe and mellow.
What is green? The grass is green,
With small flowers between.
What is violet? Clouds are violet
In the summer twilight.
What is orange? Why, an orange,
Just an orange!

Christina Rossetti

PINK

The night has come,
Pink's job is done.
She was the dawn, and the pink sun.
But now blue's time has come.
He'll be the moon,
He'll be the sky.
Pink sits and waits for sunrise,
Then she'll be the sun again,
She'll be the sky.
But sunrise won't last long.
When yellow comes
And spreads her color to the sun.
Pink sits and waits.
Pink sits and waits.

Zeynep Beler

YOU GATHER BACK THE KID

Evening
    you gather back
        all that dazzling dawn has put asunder:
            you gather a lamb
        gather a kid
gather a child to its mother

Sappho,
translated by Anne Carson

FULL MOON

She was wearing coral taffeta trousers
Someone had brought her from Isfahan,
And the little gold coat with pomegranate blossoms,
And the coral-hafted feather fan,
But she ran down a Kentish lane in the moonlight,
And skipped in the pool of moon as she ran.

She cared not a rap for all the big planets,
For Betelgeuse or Aldebaran,
And all the big planets cared nothing for her,
That small impertinent charlatan,
But she climbed on a Kentish stile in the moonlight,
And laughed at the sky through the sticks of her fan.

Vita Sackville-West

STARFISH

Went star-fishing last night.
Dipped my net in the inky lake
to catch a star for my collection.
All I did was splinter the moon.

Judith Nicholls

3.05 AM

Owl eyes
Bat wings
Moon dance
Night things.

Siana Bangura

IN A DARK STONE

"About seven thousand years ago
There was a little girl
Who looked in a mirror
And thought herself pretty."

"I don't believe you. All that time ago
If there was a little girl she'd be wild
Wearing skins, and living in damp woods."

"But seven thousand years ago
When England was a swamp with no one in it,
Long before the Romans,
In other lands by rivers and in plains
People made necklaces and learnt to write
And wrote down their accounts, and made fine pots,
Maps of the stars to sail by, and built cities;
And that is where they found this mirror
Where once the Hittite people roamed and ruled."

"So you were there, were you, all that time ago
And living far from home in ancient Turkey?"

"No, but I saw this mirror. Here in England.
It was the smallest thing in a large hall
Of great bronze cauldrons, statues, slabs of stone.
You mustn't think that it was made of glass
Common, like our mirrors.   It was
A little lump of stone, shining; black; deep;
Hard like a thick black diamond, but better: obsidian.

It would have fitted in the palm of your hand.
One side was shaped and polished, the back rough.
Small though it was I crossed the room to see it.
I wanted to look in it, to see if it worked
Really, as a mirror, but I waited."

"Why did you wait till nobody was round you?
You weren't trying to steal it were you?"
"No. I was scared.

I waited and came slowly to it sideways.
I put my hand in front. It worked as a mirror.

And then I looked into that polished stone.
I thought the shadow of the shape I looked at
Was looking out at me. My face went into
That dark deep stone and joined the other face
The pretty one that used to search her mirror
When she was alive thousands of years ago.

I don't think she'd have come if there'd been a crowd.
They were all looking at the gold and brass."

"I wish I could see it. Would she come for me?"

"I think the mirror's back in Turkey now."

"I'd travel miles and miles if I could see it."
"Well, nearer home, there were flint mines in Norfolk
And just where the land slopes a bit above some trees
On the Suffolk-Norfolk border, there's a track
And once I saw . . . But that's another story."

Jenny Joseph

FROM BOUDICCA, QUEEN OF THE ICENI, TO GAIUS SUETONIUS PAULLINUS, ON THE OCCASION OF HIS INVASION

"In stature she was very tall, in appearance most terrifying, in the glance of her eye most fierce . . ."
Cassius Dio, Roman historian

Governor! Well, what an honour –
visiting wee, cold Britannia!
Come and sit down by the fire.
Let me tell you how it works here.

Take a leg of roasted ewe.
Take a cup of steaming stew.
Take a tour and take the view.
Take your cloak off, and your shoes.

Take our lands and take our stars.
Take our jewellery, coins and furs.
Take our plough and take our horse.
Take our children from their mothers.

Take a dagger to your throat.
Take an arrow to your heart.
Take my short sword to your gut.
Take the hint, Gaius. Get out.

Kirsten Irving

SOMETIMES, CHANGE IS ONE GIRL

Sometimes, change
is just one girl with her fists clenched,
no longer willing
to be trodden on.

Elisabeth Hewer

DREAMER

roun a rocky corner
by de sea
seat up
pon a drif wood
yuh can fine she
gazin cross de water
a stick
eena her han
tryin to trace
a future
in de san

Jean Binta Breeze

DAY ONE

Today is day one of the rest of your life.
All you have to do
Is decide
What you're going to do with it.

Siana Bangura

THE BIRTH OF ISLANDS

Fire at the core
Necklace of ash, stone, coral.
Islands emerge, submerge or shift
with continental drift. Islands
are not immortal. Without you,
islands could never be. You
are the portal. Islands are born
from your longings.

See how easy:
The spoon stirs up the void
Seabird drops its egg
A sand-grain launches itself

You blow breath on the ocean

Something breaks out on the face of the water

Olive Senior

ROSA PARKS

she sorts the drawer
knives at the left
forks at the right
spoons in the middle
like neat silver petals
curved inside each other

the queue sorts itself
snaking through the bus
whites at the front
blacks at the back

but people are not knives
not forks
not spoons
their bones are full of stardust
and their hearts full of songs
and the sorting on the bus
is just plain wrong

so Rosa says no
and Rosa won't go
to the place for her race
she'll face up to all the fuss
but she's said goodbye
to the back of the bus

Jan Dean

HARRIET TUBMAN

Harriet Tubman didn't take no stuff
Wasn't scared of nothing neither
Didn't come in this world to be no slave
And wasn't going to stay one either

"Farewell!" she sang to her friends one night
She was mighty sad to leave 'em
But she ran away that dark, hot night
Ran looking for her freedom

She ran to the woods and she ran through the woods
With the slave catchers right behind her
And she kept on going till she got to the North
Where those mean men couldn't find her

Nineteen times she went back South
To get three hundred others
She ran for her freedom nineteen times
To save Black sisters and brothers
Harriet Tubman didn't take no stuff
Wasn't scared of nothing neither
Didn't come in this world to be no slave
And didn't stay one either

And didn't stay one either

Eloise Greenfield

CARVING

Others can carve out
their space
in tombs and pyramids.
Our time cannot be trapped
in cages.
Nor hope, nor laughter.
We let the moment rise
like birds and planes and angels
to the sky.

Eternity is this.
Your breath on the windowpane,
living walls with shining eyes.
The surprise of spires,
uncompromising verticals. Knowing
we have been spared
to lift our faces up
for one more day,
into one more sunrise.

Imtiaz Dharker

TO MAKE A HOMELAND

EXTRACT

Can anyone teach me
how to make a homeland?
Heartfelt thanks if you can,
heartiest thanks,
from the house-sparrows,
the apple-trees of Syria,
and yours very sincerely.

Amineh Abou Kerech,
age 13

HOW TO CUT A POMEGRANATE

"Never," said my father,
"Never cut a pomegranate
through the heart. It will weep blood.
Treat it delicately, with respect.

"Just slit the upper skin across four quarters.
This is a magic fruit,
so when you split it open, be prepared
for the jewels of the world to tumble out,
more precious than garnets,
more lustrous than rubies,
lit as if from inside.
Each jewel contains a living seed.
Separate one crystal.
Hold it up to catch the light.
Inside is a whole universe.
No common jewel can give you this."

Afterwards, I tried to make necklaces
of pomegranate seeds.
The juice spurted out, bright crimson,
and stained my fingers, then my mouth.
I didn't mind. The juice tasted of gardens
I had never seen, voluptuous
with myrtle, lemon, jasmine,
and alive with parrots' wings.

The pomegranate reminded me
that somewhere I had another home.

Imtiaz Dharker

FIRST CONTACT

The thick hair caressed her back
as she lifted her head,
And stared.

She reached her hand,
Annatto-stained, to the shoulder
Of her small dumb dog.

The parrots, for once,
Were silent,
Breaking off their bickering
To stare with her

Across the blue stillness,
To the three squares of white
Skirting the horizon.

She watched them race closer,
Big-bellied with the wind,
Saw the elaborate canoes beneath.

They were like nothing she had seen before,
So she dropped her digging stick,
And ran.

Valerie Bloom

LAMENT OF AN ARAWAK CHILD

Once I played with the hummingbirds
and sang songs to the sea.
I told my secrets to the waves
and they told theirs to me.

Now there are no more hummingbirds
and the sea songs are all sad
for strange men came and took this land
and plundered all we had.

They made my people into slaves
they worked them to the bone;
they beat them and they wore them out
now there are almost none.

Today we'll take a long canoe
and set sail on the sea
we'll steer our journey by the stars
and find a new country.

Pamela Mordecai

REMEMBER

Remember the sky that you were born under,
know each of the star's stories.
Remember the moon, know who she is.
Remember the sun's birth at dawn, that is the
strongest point of time. Remember sundown
and the giving away to night.
Remember your birth, how your mother struggled
to give you form and breath. You are evidence of
her life, and her mother's, and hers.
Remember your father. He is your life, also.
Remember the earth whose skin you are:
red earth, black earth, yellow earth, white earth
brown earth, we are earth.
Remember the plants, trees, animal life who all have their
tribes, their families, their histories, too. Talk to them,
listen to them. They are alive poems.
Remember the wind. Remember her voice. She knows the
origin of this universe.
Remember you are all people and all people
are you.
Remember you are this universe and this
universe is you.
Remember all is in motion, is growing, is you.
Remember language comes from this.
Remember the dance language is, that life is.
Remember.

Joy Harjo

SEA TIMELESS SONG

Hurricane come
and hurricane go
but sea . . . sea timeless
sea timeless
sea timeless
sea timeless
sea timeless

Hibiscus bloom
then dry-wither so
but sea . . . sea timeless
sea timeless
sea timeless
sea timeless
sea timeless

Tourist come
and tourist go
but sea . . . sea timeless
sea timeless
sea timeless
sea timeless
sea timeless

Grace Nichols

LOW-TIDE

These wet rocks where the tide has been,
  Barnacled white and weeded brown
And slimed beneath to a beautiful green,
  These wet rocks where the tide went down
Will show again when the tide is high
  Faint and perilous, far from shore,
No place to dream, but a place to die:
  The bottom of the sea once more.

There was a child that wandered through
  A giant's empty house all day –
House full of wonderful things and new,
  But no fit place for a child to play!

Edna St Vincent Millay

SELKIE

The secret me is a boy.

He takes girlness off like a sealskin:
something that never sat right on his shoulders.

The secret me is broad-shouldered;
the sea can't contain him,

the land can't anchor his waves
to its sand.

The secret me swims
with the big fish, brash, he swaggers

like a mermaid, bares teeth
like daggers, barks at the moon when it's thin.

He's whiskered, that boy. Thick-skinned.
Quick-finned, always turning tail.

He wears his own skin like a sail,
lets it carry him to where

salt swallows mouthfuls of air.
Let them find me there by the shore:

The girl-seal with a secret
boy inside. Rough-voiced. Black-eyed.

Washed bare
as the beach by the tide.

Rachel Plummer

I STARTED EARLY – TOOK MY DOG –

I started Early – Took my Dog –
And visited the Sea –
The Mermaids in the Basement
Came out to look at me –

And Frigates – in the Upper Floor
Extended Hempen Hands –
Presuming Me to be a Mouse –
Aground – upon the Sands –

But no Man moved Me – till the Tide
Went past my simple Shoe –
And past my Apron – and my Belt
And past my Bodice – too –

And made as He would eat me up –
As wholly as a Dew
Upon a Dandelion's Sleeve –
And then – I started – too –

And He – He followed – close behind –
I felt His Silver Heel
Upon my Ankle – Then my Shoes
Would overflow with Pearl –

Until We met the Solid Town –
No One He seemed to know –
And bowing – with a Mighty look –
At me – The Sea withdrew –

Emily Dickinson

SISTER IN A WHALE

You live in the hollow of a stranded whale
lying on top of our house.
My father was embarrassed by this
so a roof was put up as camouflage.
On the ribs you have hung plants
and a miniature replica of a whale
to remind you where you are.
The stomach lining is plastered with posters
and your *Snoopy for President* buttons
are stuck to a piece of blubber beside your bed.
Through the spout you observe cloud formations.
It isn't as orderly as a regular room:
it's more like a shipwreck of notebooks,
school projects, shirts, paper bags,
coke cans, photographs and magazines
that has been washed up with the tide.
You beachcomb every morning for something to wear;
then it's down the corkscrew
to the real world.

Julie O'Callaghan

IN ISAS BED

I love in Isas bed to lie
O such a joy and luxury
The bottom of the bed I sleep*
And with great care I myself keep
Oft I embrace her feet of lillys
But she has goton all the pillies.
Her neck I never can embrace
But I do hug her feet in place
But I am sure I am contented
And of my follies am repented
I am sure I'd rather be
In a small bed at liberty

Marjory Fleming, age 6

* *Note by the poet: "I disturbed her repose at night by contunial figiting and kicking but I was very contunialy at work reading the Arabin nights entertainments which I could not have done had I slept at the top."*

BED TIME

Can i stay up five
minutes more let me
finish this book
Can't I finish this
bead chain
Can't I finish this
castle
        Can't I
        stay up
five minutes or four
three minutes or two
minutes one minute more.

Accabre Huntley

THE PLEIADES

By day you cannot see the sky
For it is up so very high.
You look and look, but it's so blue
That you can never see right through.

But when night comes it is quite plain,
And all the stars are there again.
They seem just like old friends to me,
I've known them all my life you see.

There is the dipper first, and there
Is Cassiopeia in her chair,
Orion's belt, the Milky Way,
And lots I know but cannot say.

One group looks like a swarm of bees,
Papa says they're the Pleiades;
But I think they must be the toy
Of some nice little angel boy.

Perhaps his jackstones which today
He has forgot to put away,
And left them lying on the sky
Where he will find them by and by.

I wish he'd come and play with me.
We'd have such fun, for it would be
A most unusual thing for boys
To feel that they had stars for toys!

Amy Lowell

LULLABY

If I could write some music for the rain
To play upon your nursery windowpane
You'd sleep the sounder for its lullaby
And it would sing more tunefully than I.

If I could teach the clock to tell you tales
Of unicorns and ships with silver sails
You'd never hear the story fail and die
For clocks don't tend to nod as much as I.

If I could knit the shadows into shawls,
Unpick bad dreams and wind them into balls,
We'd throw them through the window at the sky,
Then pull the darkness round us, you and I.

Sue Cowling

DANCING

Wide sleeves sway.
Scents,
Sweet scents
Incessantly coming.
It is red lilies,
Lotus lilies,
Floating up,
And up,
Out of Autumn mist.
Thin clouds
Puffed,
Fluttered,
Blown on a rippling wind
Through a mountain pass.
Young willow shoots
Touching,
Brushing,
The water
Of the garden pool.

Yang Kuei-Fei

BLIZZARD

the snow
has forgotten
how to stop
it falls
stuttering
at the glass
a silk windsock
of snow
blowing
under the porch light
tangling trees
which bend
like old women
snarled
in their own
knitting
snow drifts
up to the step
over the doorsill
a pointillist's blur
the wedding
of form and motion
shaping itself
to the wish of
any object it touches
chairs become
laps of snow
the moon could be
breaking apart
and falling
over the eaves
over the roof
a white bear
shaking its paw
at the window
splitting the hive
of winter
snow stinging
the air
I pull a comforter
of snow
up to my chin
and tumble
to sleep
as the whole
alphabet
of silence
falls out of the
sky

Linda Pastan

WINTER POEM

once a snowflake fell
on my brow and i loved
it so much and i kissed
it and it was happy and called its cousins
and brothers and a web
of snow engulfed me then
i reached to love them all
and i squeezed them and they became
a spring rain and i stood perfectly
still and was a flower

Nikki Giovanni

LOOKING FORWARD

The days are getting longer.
From my first-floor window
I can sit and watch
the tide of people ebb and flow
I know them all
the early-morning milkman
postman
paperboy
the schoolchild
worker
shopper.
I invent their lives.
Now I have started looking forward
to the sights and sounds
of summer evenings
by my open window
children playing late
lawnmowers
couples walking dogs.
And yet
perhaps this summer I shall not be here.
My days are getting shorter.

Sue Cowling

GREEN RAIN

Into the scented woods we'll go,
And see the blackthorn swim in snow.
High above, in the budding leaves,
A brooding dove awakes and grieves;
The glades with mingled music stir,
And wildly laughs the woodpecker.
When blackthorn petals pearl the breeze,
There are the twisted hawthorn trees
Thick-set with buds, as clear and pale
As golden water or green hail—
As if a storm of rain had stood
Enchanted in the thorny wood,
And, hearing fairy voices call,
Hung poised, forgetting how to fall.

Mary Webb

COLOURING IN

And staying inside the lines
Is fine, but . . .
I like it when stuff leaks—
When the blue bird and the blue sky
Are just one blur of blue blue flying,
And the feeling of the feathers in the air
And the wind along the blade of wing
Is a long gash of smudgy colour.
I like it when the flowers and the sunshine
Puddle red and yellow into orange,
The way the hot sun on my back
Lulls me—muddles me—sleepy
In the scented garden,
Makes me part of the picture . . .
Part of the place.

Jan Dean

THE SUMMER DAY

Who made the world?
Who made the swan, and the black bear?
Who made the grasshopper?
This grasshopper, I mean –
the one who has flung herself out of the grass,
the one who is eating sugar out of my hand,
who is moving her jaws back and forth instead of up and down –
who is gazing around with her enormous and complicated eyes.
Now she lifts her pale forearms and thoroughly washes her face.
Now she snaps her wings open, and floats away.
I don't know exactly what a prayer is.
I do know how to pay attention, how to fall down
into the grass, how to kneel down in the grass,
how to be idle and blessed, how to stroll through the fields,
which is what I have been doing all day.
Tell me, what else should I have done?
Doesn't everything die at last, and too soon?
Tell me, what is it you plan to do
with your one wild and precious life?

Mary Oliver

WANTED: WORLD-SITTER

WANTED: sitter
to care for this
elderly world:
to look after
all its many needs,

to keep it going
until its last day,
the extinction
of all its life.
You must stop it

becoming too warm
as this just leads
to storms and floods
of tears and to
so much damage.

You will not be
liked. All of us
comfortable
people will hate
all that you say.

Susanna Dalton

ON FORGETTING THAT I AM A TREE

A poem in which I am growing.

A poem in which I am a tree,
And I am both appreciated and undervalued.

A poem in which I fear I did not dig into the past,
Did not think about my roots,
Forgot what it meant to be planted.

A poem in which I realize they may try to cut me down,
That I must change with the seasons,
That I do it so well
It looks like they are changing with me.

A poem in which I remember I have existed for centuries,
That centuries are far too small a unit of measurement,
That time found itself in the forests, woods and jungles.
Remember I have witnessed creation,
That I am key to it.

A poem in which some will carve their names into my skin
In hopes the universe will know them.
Where I am so tall I kiss the sun.
Trees cannot hide,
They belong to the day and to the night,
To the past and the future.

A poem in which I stop looking for it,
Because I am home.
I am habitat.
My branches are host and shelter
I am life-giver and fruit-bearer.
Self-sufficient protection.

A poem in which I remember I am a tree.

Ruth Awolola

CANCAN

When I dance
my blood runs like a river can,
my feet fly like the birds can,
my heart beats like a drum can.
Because when I dance I can,
can do anything
when I dance.

Flying over rooftops
I see my town below me
where everybody knows me,
where all my problems throw me,
where heavy feet can slow me.
But nobody can, can stop me
when I dance.

My blood runs a race.
My feet fly in space.
My heart beats the pace.
Because when I dance I can,
can do anything
when I dance.

Mandy Coe

YOUR GRANDMOTHER

Remember, remember, there's many a thing
your grandmother doesn't dig
if it ain't got that swing;
many a piece of swag
she won't pick up and put in her bag
if it seems like a drag.
She painted it red – the town –
she lassooed the moon.
Remember, remember, your grandmother
boogied on down.

Remember, remember, although your grandmother's old,
she shook, she rattled, she rolled.
She was so cool she was cold,
she was solid gold.
Your grandmother played it neat,
wore two little blue suede shoes
on her dancing feet –
oo, reet-a-teet-teet –
Remember, remember, your grandmother
got with the beat.

Remember, remember, it ain't what you do
it's the way that you do it.
Your grandmother knew it –
she had a balloon and she blew it,
she had a ball
and was belle of it
just for the hell of it.
She was Queen of the night.
Remember, remember, your grandmother's
aaaaaaaaaaaallllllll riiiiiiiiiiiiiiiight.

Carol Ann Duffy

EIGHTEENTH CENTURY LADY

Oh, she was a lady all alive!
She bedeviled the beaux
who would woo and wive;
she wore no sackcloth
and no ashes,
she wore beads
and Persian sashes.
She wore feathers
and fine fancies
going to routs
and plays and dances,
with gewgaws, whims
and silver dresses,
and pearls and curls
and twirls of tresses.
Her jewels shone
like midnight's marchers,
her hair built high
as Lady's Archer's,
with brooches, wings
and wonders wiry.
Her witchy face
was fine and fiery.
Her hoop it nearly
spread an acre;
she was a credit
to her maker.
Her maker was pleased
he could contrive
such a lady,
a lady all alive.

Rose O'Neill

MISTRESS COOPER

A hat-fanatic, a hat-fanatic,
Mistress Cooper is a hat-fanatic,
every hat she sees she has to have it.
Who knows how she got the hat-habit.

High hats, low hats,
fat hats, skinny hats,
springy hats, frilly hats,
cocky hats, floppy hats.
Hats in hat-boxes, hats on hat-racks,
a hundred and twenty-two to be exact.

"How's that for a hat?" she'll say to you,
whenever she wears a hat that is new.
If you value the friendship of Mistress Cooper
simply answer, "It's super-dooper."

Grace Nichols

LIKE A SUN

Imagine. It's daybreak. You're only eighteen,
and somebody says "Now it's time to be queen."
You stir in your blankets. Who *was* it that spoke?
You're still half asleep. Was it some sort of joke?

Queen? I mean, *really*? You're daydreaming it, right?
Then the curtains are opened, and in that faint light
stands your mother, who says "Now, there's no time to dress",
so you get out of bed, with your hair still a mess,

and you walk down the cold empty length of the hall
all alone in the world, feeling lost and as small
as a pinprick star in the black of the sky.
But a queen, like a sun, must be born, by and by.

I know who you are, though I'm long since dead.
I've seen all you've done, and I've heard all you've said.
So I guess now you're chatting, or playing with apps,
or reading, or singing, or dancing, perhaps,

and your life's like a promise, a blank new page
that is open and free, not a palace-shaped cage.
You can learn, you can earn, be with friends, stay up late.
Not burdened at birth by some pre-decreed fate,

or bound by the coils of the old golden chain
of honour and duty and history, to reign.
I have to accept, but I want to scream "WHY?"
Yet a queen, like a sun, must rise, by and by.

Imagine. They tell you your uncle has died.
He was old, he was ill, but you're crying inside,
not only for him, but your childhood too,
and all of those things that you wanted to do.

There is so much in life that you don't understand,
so how will you manage to rule the whole land?
Meet ministers, lords . . . can't this wait? Not today.
You're still far too young! Oh, but what can you say?

So you put on a smile, and you tidy your frown.
You watch as the people around you bow down,
then you take up the crown, and you hold your head high.
For a queen, like a sun, must blaze, by and by.

Elli Woollard

Blinding the north as it went by,
Too burning and too quick to hold,
Too lovely to be bought or sold,
Good only to make wishes on
And then forever to be gone.

Sara Teasdale

LODESTAR

Here is what I believe
will be the hardest thing
to do:
to remember
that we have
a soul.
It is so quiet
the soul
and weighs
almost nothing.
It might flash
across
our dullest days
only once or twice
in a lifetime.
That it is there:
just the certainty
of knowing
must be
our lodestar.

Alice Walker

CHIMES

Brief, on a flying night
    From the shaken tower,
A flock of bells take flight,
    And go with the hour.

Like birds from the cote to the gales,
    Abrupt – O hark!
A fleet of bells set sails,
    And go to the dark.

Sudden the cold airs swing,
    Alone, aloud,
A verse of bells takes wing
    And flies with the cloud.

Alice Meynell

DON'T BE SCARED

The dark is only a blanket
for the moon to put on her bed.

The dark is a private cinema
for the movie dreams in your head.

The dark is a little black dress
to show off the sequin stars.

The dark is the wooden hole
behind the strings of happy guitars.

The dark is a jeweller's velvet cloth
where children sleep like pearls.

The dark is a spool of film
to photograph boys and girls,

so smile in your sleep in the dark.
Don't be scared.

Carol Ann Duffy

I LIKE TO STAY UP

I like to stay up
and listen
when big people talking
jumbie* stories

I does feel
so tingly and excited
inside me

But when my mother say
“Girl, time for bed”

Then is when
I does feel a dread

Then is when
I does cover up
from me feet to me head

Then is when
I does wish I didn’t listen
to no stupid jumbie story

Then is when
I does wish I did read
me book instead

Grace Nichols

* *Jumbie – Guyanese word for “ghost”*

WHY IS IT?

Why is it that the taps all drip,
The electricity wires trip,
Tired pipes in the attic grumble,
Empty washer-dryers tumble,
Floorboards creak and old joints moan,
Doorposts squeak and rafters groan,
Fridges softly hum and sigh,
Cats out in the garden cry
Like a band of mad banshees,
The wind howls eerily in the trees,
The telephone rings, there's no one there,
There are soft whispers in the air,
The moon starts playing hide and seek,
Your head feels light, you knees feel weak,
You think you're not alone in bed,
And wish you were elsewhere instead,

When you're alone at night?

Valerie Bloom

FRAGMENT FOR THE DARK

Let it not come near me, let it not
Fold round or over me. One weak hand
Clutches a foot of air, asks the brisk buds
To suffer grey winds, spear through
Fog I feel in me. Give me the magic
To see grounded starlings, their polish
As this threat of all-day night. Mind, mind
In me, make thoughts candles to light me
Out of the furthest reach of possible nights.
Lantern me, stars, if I look up through wet hands,
Show assurance in blurred shining. I have
Put every light in the house on.
May their filaments last till true morning.

Elizabeth Jennings

SMALL AIRCRAFT

As if I didn't have enough
Bothering me, now I'm confused
By dreaming nightly
Of small airplanes. I don't understand it.

The planes don't care that I dream of them:
Now like chickens they peck seed
From my hand. Now like termites
They live in the walls of my house.

Or else they poke me
With their dumb noses: little fish
Move like this to a child's foot,
Tickling, making their feet laugh.

Sometimes they push and bump each other
Around my fire, blinded by the light.
They won't let me read and the noise
Of their wings excites me.

They have another trick: they come
To me like children in tears
And sit in my lap,
Crying, *Take us in your arms.*

You can drive them away, but they're right back,
Flying out of the polished darkness,
Looking out from their eyes like sad dachshunds
As their long bodies float by.

Bella Akhmadulina,
translated by Daniel Halpern

WHEREVER

Here she comes
whisper the trees
boughs sway heavy
with gossiping leaves

Where will she go?
murmur the breezes

However, whenever
wherever she pleases

Here she comes
whispers the sea
droplets colliding
with gossipy glee

Where will she go?
murmurs the sand

However, whenever
wherever she can

Here she comes
whispers the river
gossip like ripples
disperse with a quiver

Where will she go?
murmur the reeds

However, whenever
wherever she needs.

Jackie Hosking

GHOST IN THE GARDEN

The ghost in the garden
Cracks twigs as she treads
Shuffles the leaves
But isn't there

The ghost in the garden
Snaps back the brambles
So they spring against my legs
But isn't there

Draws spiders' webs across my face
Breathes mist on my cheek
Whispers with bird-breath down my ear
But isn't there

Tosses raindrops down from branches
Splashes the pond
Traces a face in it
That isn't mine

Moves shadows underneath the trees
Too tall, too thin, too tiny to be me
Spreads bindweed out to catch me
Flutters wild wings about my head
Tugs at my hair
But isn't there

And when I look
There's only the bend of grass
Where her running feet
Have smudged the dew

And there's only the sigh
Of her laughter
Trickling
Like
Moonlight
On
Wet
Weeds.

Berlie Doherty

BRAVE ENOUGH

I wonder would you be my closest friend
if I was brave enough
to tie the ribbons of your dress to mine
and run like girl and shadow, shade and girl,
across the grass.

                    I wonder
would you climb into this tree
if I was brave enough to toss an apple down
from where I watch you on your way to school
and sit beside me on the branch

                              swinging your legs
as, brave enough, I'd say *Let's stay*
forever in this tree, girl and shadow, shade and girl,
you and me, and not grow older, richer, wiser, sadder
by one day. I wonder what you'd say.

Carol Ann Duffy

WHEN I WAS A BIRD

I climbed up the karaka tree
Into a nest all made of leaves
But soft as feathers
I made up a song that went on singing all by itself
And hadn't any words but got sad at the end.
There were daisies in the grass under the tree.
I said, just to try them:
"I'll bite off your heads and give them to my little children to eat."
But they didn't believe I was a bird
They stayed quite open.
The sky was like a blue nest with white feathers
And the sun was the mother bird keeping it warm.
That's what my song said: though it hadn't any words.
Little Brother came up the path, wheeling his barrow
I made my dress into wings and kept very quiet
Then when he was quite near I said: "sweet – sweet."
For a moment he looked quite startled –
Then he said: "Pooh, you're not a bird; I can see your legs."
But the daisies didn't really matter
And Little Brother didn't really matter –
I felt *just* like a bird.

Katherine Mansfield

IT WAS LONG AGO

I'll tell you, shall I, something I remember?
Something that still means a great deal to me.
It was long ago.

A dusty road in summer I remember,
A mountain, and an old house, and a tree
That stood, you know,

Behind the house. An old woman I remember
In a red shawl with a grey cat on her knee
Humming under a tree.

She seemed the oldest thing I can remember,
But then perhaps I was not more than three.
It was long ago.

I dragged on the dusty road, and I remember
How the old woman looked over the fence at me
And seemed to know

How it felt to be three, and called out, I remember
"Do you like bilberries and cream for tea?"
I went under the tree

And while she hummed, and the cat purred, I remember
How she filled a saucer with berries and cream for me
So long ago,

Such berries and such cream as I remember
I never had seen before, and never see
Today, you know.

And that is almost all I can remember,
The house, the mountain, the grey cat on her knee,
Her red shawl, and the tree,

And the taste of the berries, the feel of the sun I remember,
And the smell of everything that used to be
So long ago,

Till the heat on the road outside again I remember,
And how the long dusty road seemed to have for me
No end, you know.

That is the farthest thing I can remember.
It won't mean much to you. It does to me.
Then I grew up, you see.

Eleanor Farjeon

AN OLD WOMAN'S FIRE

I remember watching my grandmother build her fire
The honest kindling, the twisted newspaper,
The tiny tower of good black coal.
And how, once lit, she'd hold a sheet of newspaper
Across the fire and say, "Watch it suck, dear."

I remember the way my grandmother loved to poke her fire
Always nudging the coals and turning them over
opening the grate, placing another jet jewel on the glowing fire
and how she'd fuss over the dying embers.

I remember how she sat there in her armchair,
Her old face, a little pink and flushed from the heat.
And how she'd smile at her coal fire, lovingly,
And sigh, "There's nothing like a real fire is there dear?"

As if her life could have been something else entirely.

Jackie Kay

TWO OLD WOMEN

The two of us sit in the doorway
chatting about our children and grandchildren.
We sink happily
into our oldwomanhood.

Like two spoons
sinking
into a bowl of hot porridge.

Anna 'Swir'

A SUITCASE OF SEAWEED

Across the ocean
from Korea
my grandmother,
my Halmoni,
has come –
her suitcase
sealed shut
with tape,
packed full
of sheets
of shiny black
seaweed
and stacks
of dried squid.
We break it open,
this old treasure
chest of hers,
holding
our noses
tight
as we release
its ripe
sea smell.

Janet S. Wong

GRANDPA'S SOUP

No one makes soup like my Grandpa's,
with its diced carrots the perfect size
and its diced potatoes the perfect size
and its wee soft bits –
what are their names?
and its big bit of hough,
which rhymes with loch, floating
like a rich island in the middle of the soup sea.

I say, Grandpa, Grandpa your soup is the best soup in the whole world.
And Grandpa says, Och,
which rhymes with hough and loch,
Och, Don't be daft,
because he's shy about his soup, my Grandpa.
He knows I will grow up and pine for it.
I will fall ill and desperately need it.
I will long for it my whole life after he is gone.
Every soup will become sad and wrong after he is gone.
He knows when I'm older I will avoid soup altogether.
Oh Grandpa, Grandpa, why is your soup so glorious? I say
tucking into my fourth bowl in a day.

Barley! That's the name of the wee soft bit. Barley.

Jackie Kay

SOUP

From the lighted window
I watch my mother
picking leeks in twilight.

I will have soup
for my supper,
sprinkled with green parsley.

She passes me my creamy bowl.
My hands are warm,
and smell of soap.

My mother's hands are cold as roots.
She shuts up the chickens
by moonlight.

Selima Hill

SOUP
EXTRACT

And we forget to sing
We forget to celebrate that we are one
That the act of love was the sitting down together
And sharing the pot of soup in the first place

Salena Godden

SPELL OF THE BRIDGE

Hold the wish on your tongue
As you cross
What the bridge cannot hear
Cannot fall

For the river would carry
Your hopes to the sea
To the net of a stranger
To the silt bed of dreams

Hold the wish on your tongue
As you cross
And on the far side
Let the wish go first

Helen Lamb

YOU'RE STILL GOING

You're still going.
And that's the thing, isn't it?
Despite it all,
despite this big cruel world –
you're still going.

Elisabeth Hewer

QUESTIONS

EXTRACT

What are you?
I'm a person, just like you.
Look: two eyes, two ears, a mouth, a nose.
I eat, I sleep, I laugh, I weep;
what other label
would you put on me?

Elaine Gallagher

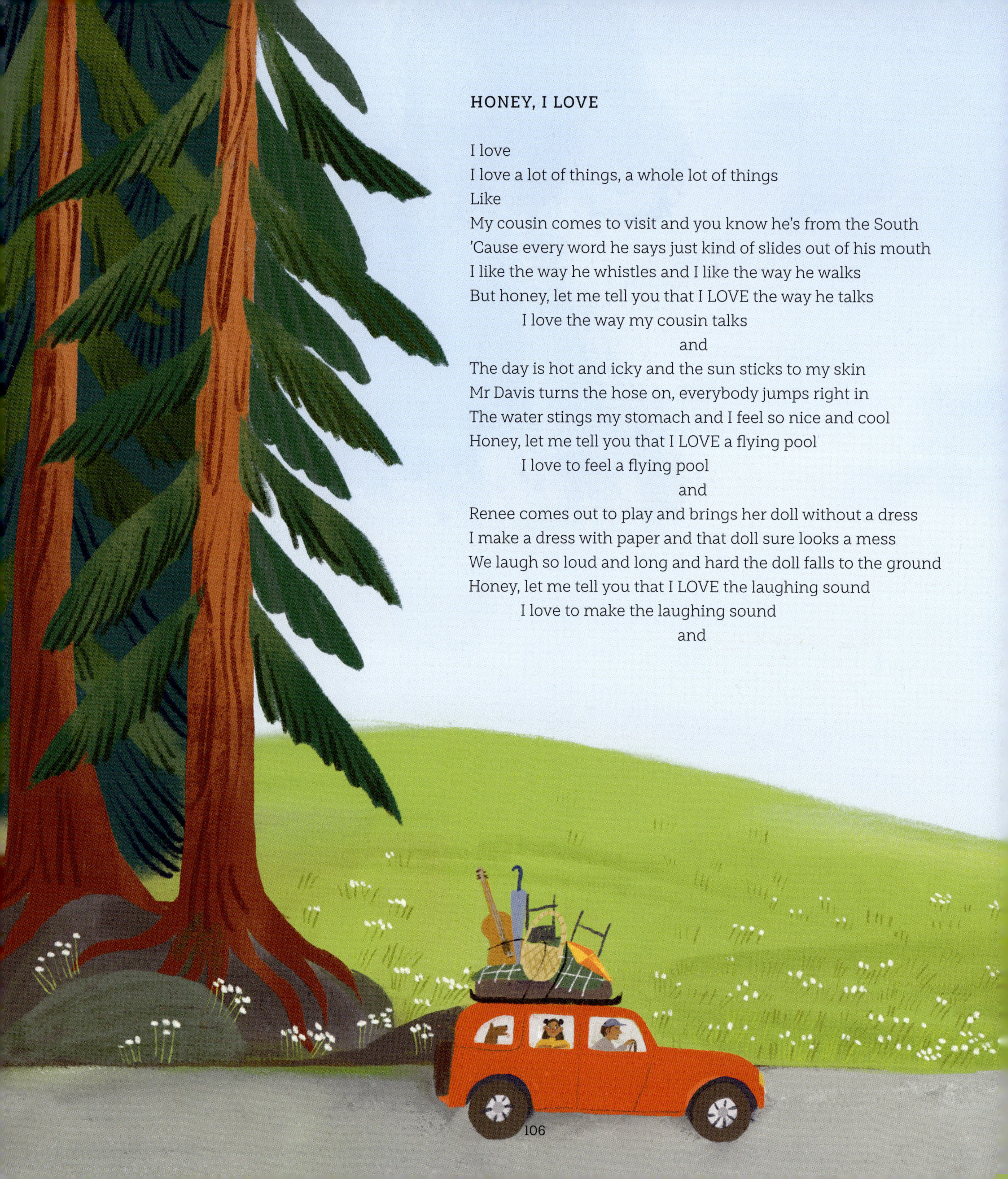

HONEY, I LOVE

I love
I love a lot of things, a whole lot of things
Like
My cousin comes to visit and you know he's from the South
'Cause every word he says just kind of slides out of his mouth
I like the way he whistles and I like the way he walks
But honey, let me tell you that I LOVE the way he talks
I love the way my cousin talks
and
The day is hot and icky and the sun sticks to my skin
Mr Davis turns the hose on, everybody jumps right in
The water stings my stomach and I feel so nice and cool
Honey, let me tell you that I LOVE a flying pool
I love to feel a flying pool
and
Renee comes out to play and brings her doll without a dress
I make a dress with paper and that doll sure looks a mess
We laugh so loud and long and hard the doll falls to the ground
Honey, let me tell you that I LOVE the laughing sound
I love to make the laughing sound
and

My uncle's car is crowded and there's a lot of food to eat
We're going down the country where the church folks like to meet
I'm looking out the window at the cows and trees outside
Honey, let me tell you that I LOVE to take a ride
I just love to take a family ride
and
My mama's on the sofa sewing buttons on my coat
I go and sit beside her, I'm through playing with my boat
I hold her arm and kiss it, 'cause it feels so soft and warm
Honey, let me tell you that I LOVE my mama's arm
I love to kiss my mama's arm
and
It's not so late at night, but still I'm lying in my bed
I guess I need my rest, at least that's what my mama said
She told me not to cry 'cause she don't want to hear a peep
Honey, let me tell you I DON'T love to go to sleep
I do not love to go to sleep
But I love
I love a lot of things, a whole lot of things
And honey,
I love you, too.

Eloise Greenfield

EVERYDAY THINGS

Millionaires, presidents – even kings
Can't get along without everyday things.

Were you president, king or millionaire,
You'd use a comb to comb your hair.

If you wished to be clean – and you would, I hope –
You'd take a bath with water and soap.

And you'd have to eat – if you wanted to eat –
Bread and vegetables, fish and meat;

While your drink for breakfast would probably be
Milk or chocolate, coffee or tea.

You'd have to wear – you could hardly refuse –
Under clothes, outer clothes, stockings and shoes.

If you wished to make a reminding note,
You'd take a pencil out of your coat;

And you couldn't sign a letter, I think,
With anything better than pen and ink.

If you wanted to read, you'd be sure to look
At newspaper, magazine, or book;

And if it happened that you were ill,
You'd down some oil or choke on a pill.

If you had a cold I can only suppose
You'd use a handkerchief for your nose.

When you wanted to rest your weary head,
Like other folks, you'd hop into bed.

Millionaires, presidents – even kings
Can't get along without everyday things.

Jean Ayer

BREAKFAST FOR ONE

Hot thick crusty buttery toast
Buttery toasty thick hot crust
Crusty buttery hot thick toast
Crusty thick hot toasty butter
Thick hot buttery crusty toast
Toasty buttery hot thick crust
Hot buttery thick crusty toast—

With marmalade is how I like it most!

Judith Nicholls

DOG

Best friend?
Maybe!
Wiry hair-dropper,
four-legged yapper.
Sleep-disturber,
paws on the shoulders
and lick on the chin.
Unruly friend, sometimes.
I remember
Great Dane,
lolloping up stairs,
five-at-a-time
then sitting,
patient King of the Castle,
waiting for his slow
two-legged servant,
panting below.
Best friend!

Judith Nicholls

TIPSY

A small cat
climbs into my lap;
the one who usually
keeps her distance.
I cradle her,
chin resting on my arm,
purr barely a quiver
against my hand,
while my coffee
grows cold.

Elaine Gallagher

TABBY

My cat is all concentrated tiger.
I can only imagine the thousands
of millions of years
it must have taken to perfect her.
Growing smaller and smaller
with each evolution.
Growing more and more refined
and even-tempered under her fur.

See how she constantly licks
and grooms herself all over?

A small Queen of Sheba
stamping everywhere her padded
signature – a royal reminder
of the days she was a full-blown tiger.
Older O much older than Egypt.

Now, just look at her –
My grey and black tabby, stepping lightly,
emerging head first from between
the green garden stalks –

Ancient and new as the birth of a star.

Grace Nichols

CATS

Cats sleep
Anywhere,
Any table,
Any chair,
Top of piano,
Window ledge,
In the middle,
On the edge,
Open drawer,
Empty shoe,
Anybody's
Lap will do,
Fitted in a
Cardboard box,
In the cupboard
With your frocks—
Anywhere!
They don't care!
Cats sleep
Anywhere.

Eleanor Farjeon

TREASURE TROVE

I have a tin
to keep things in
underneath
my bedroom floor.

I put my finger
in the crack,
quietly lift
the floorboard back,

and there's my store,
safely hid
in a tin with roses
on the lid.

A few feathers
and a chicken's claw,
a big tooth
from a dinosaur,

the wrapper
from my Easter Egg,
a Christmas robin
with one leg,

long hairs
from a horse's mane,
real pesetas
come from Spain,

three of my
operation stitches,
like spiders
wrapped in bandages,

a marble
full of dragon smoke,
flashing with fire
in the dark,

a magic pebble
round and white,
a sparkler left
from Bonfire Night.

Underneath
my bedroom floor
there's a treasure tin,
with my things in.

Irene Rawnsley

KEEP A POEM IN YOUR POCKET

Keep a poem in your pocket
and a picture in your head
and you'll never feel lonely
at night when you're in bed.

The little poem will sing to you
the little picture bring to you
a dozen dreams to dance to you
at night when you're in bed.

So –
Keep a picture in your pocket
and a poem in your head
and you'll never feel lonely
at night when you're in bed.

Beatrice Schenk de Regniers

ADMONITIONS

EXTRACT

children
when they ask you
why is your mama so funny
say
she is a poet
she don't have no sense

Lucille Clifton

IN MY DREAMS

In my dreams I am always saying goodbye and riding away,
Whither and why I know not nor do I care.
And the parting is sweet and the parting over is sweeter,
And sweetest of all is the night and the rushing air.

In my dreams they are always waving their hands and saying goodbye,
And they give me the stirrup cup and I smile as I drink,
I am glad the journey is set, I am glad I am going,
I am glad, I am glad, that my friends don't know what I think.

Stevie Smith

THE FEMALE HIGHWAYMAN

Priscilla on one summer's day
Dressed herself up in men's array;
With a brace of pistols by her side
All for to meet her true love she did ride.

And when she saw her true love there
She boldly bade him for to stand.
"Stand and deliver, kind sir," she said,
"For if you don't I'll shoot you dead."

And when she'd robbed him of all his store,
Said she, "Kind sir, there's one thing more;
The diamond ring I've seen you wear,
Deliver that and your life I'll spare."

"That ring," said he, "my true love gave;
My life I'll lose but that I'll save."
Then, being tender-hearted like a dove,
She rode away from the man she love.

Anon they walked upon the green,
And he spied his watch pinned to her clothes,
Which made her blush, which made her blush
Like a full, blooming rose.

"'Twas me who robbed you on the plain,
So here's your watch and your gold again.
I did it only for to see
If you would really faithful be.
And now I'm sure that this is true,
I also give my heart to you."

Anonymous

I MAY, I MIGHT, I MUST

If you will tell me why the fen
appears impassable, I then
will tell you why I think that I
can get across it if I try.

Marianne Moore

THE CENTAUR

The summer that I was ten—
Can it be there was only one
summer that I was ten? It must

have been a long one then—
each day I'd go out to choose
a fresh horse from my stable

which was a willow grove
down by the old canal.
I'd go on my two bare feet.

But when, with my brother's jack-knife,
I had cut me a long limber horse
with a good thick knob for a head,

and peeled him slick and clean
except a few leaves for the tail,
and cinched my brother's belt

around his head for a rein,
I'd straddle and canter him fast
up the grass bank to the path,

trot along in the lovely dust
that talcumed over his hoofs,
hiding my toes, and turning

his feet to swift half-moons.
The willow knob with the strap
jouncing between my thighs

was the pommel and yet the poll
of my nickering pony's head.
My head and my neck were mine,

yet they were shaped like a horse.
My hair flopped to the side
like the mane of a horse in the wind.

My forelock swung in my eyes,
my neck arched and I snorted.
I shied and skittered and reared,

stopped and raised my knees,
pawed at the ground and quivered.
My teeth bared as we wheeled

and swished through the dust again.
I was the horse and the rider,
and the leather I slapped to his rump

spanked my own behind.
Doubled, my two hoofs beat
a gallop along the bank,

the wind twanged in my mane,
my mouth squared to the bit.
And yet I sat on my steed

quiet, negligent riding,
my toes standing the stirrups,
my thighs hugging his ribs.

At a walk we drew up to the porch.
I tethered him to a paling.
Dismounting, I smoothed my skirt

and entered the dusky hall.
My feet on the clean linoleum
left ghostly toes in the hall.

Where have you been? said my mother.
Been riding, I said from the sink,
and filled me a glass of water.

What's that in your pocket? she said.
Just my knife. It weighted my pocket
and stretched my dress awry.

Go tie back your hair, said my mother,
and *Why is your mouth all green?*
Rob Roy, he pulled some clover
as we crossed the field, I told her.

May Swenson

MOONLILY

When we play horses at recess, my name
is Moonlily and I'm a yearling mare.
We gallop circles around the playground,
whinnying, neighing, and shaking our manes.
We scrape the ground with scuffed saddle oxfords,
thunder around the little kids on swings
and seesaws, and around the boys' ball games.
We're sorrel, chestnut, buckskin, pinto, gray,
a herd in pastel dresses and white socks.
We're self-named, untamed, untouched, unridden.
Our plains know no fences. We can smell spring.
The bell produces metamorphosis.
Still hot and flushed, we file back to our desks,
one bay in a room of palominos.

Marilyn Nelson

HOW TO TRIUMPH LIKE A GIRL

I like the lady horses best,
how they make it all look easy,
like running 40 miles per hour
is as fun as taking a nap, or grass.
I like their lady horse swagger,
after winning. Ears up, girls, ears up!
But mainly, let's be honest, I like
that they're ladies. As if this big
dangerous animal is also part of me,
that somewhere inside the delicate
skin of my body, there pumps
an 8-pound female horse heart,
giant with power, heavy with blood.
Don't you want to believe it?
Don't you want to lift my shirt and see
the huge beating genius machine
that thinks, no, it knows,
it's going to come in first.

Ada Limón

YOU CAN CHANGE THE WORLD
GIRLS
GIRLS
HONOUR LOVE, RESPECT WOMEN
GRL
GIRLS support GIRLS

"A WOMAN'S PLACE"

EXTRACT

i heard a woman becomes herself
the first time she speaks
without permission

then, every word out of her mouth
a riot

say, *beautiful*
& point to the map of your body
say, *brave*
& wear your skin like a gown or a suit
say, *hero*
& cast yourself in the lead role

Denice Frohman

HERE ARE GIRLS LIKE LIONS

Here are girls like lions,
here are girls like howling wolves.
Here are girls with such big teeth!
Here are girls who'll play tug o' war
with your heart or your wishbone
Or your throat, oh.

Oh, here are girls
with cold bright eyes and claws
like dragons. Here are girls who
can't breathe air, only fire.
Here are girls who carry kindness
And katanas in their rucksacks
because they never know which they'll need.

How do you tame girls with wildfire limbs?
How do you hold down girls with hurricane hands?

Oh, you can't. Humble hungerer,
you've just got to help them rise.

Elisabeth Hewer

MALALA

A girl with a book.
A girl with a book.
That's what has scared them –
A girl, with a book.

They get on to the bus.
They call out my name.
They aim. And they fire.
A shot to the brain.

Because a girl with a book,
A girl with a voice,
A girl with a brain,
A girl with a choice,
A girl with a plan
To have rights, like a man.
That's what they're scared of,
One girl, with a book.

A girl who has words.
A girl with a pen.
A girl to be heard
With support of her friends
Who want to live free –
That's what they fear,
A girl just like me.

Michaela Morgan

LIFE DOESN'T FRIGHTEN ME

Shadows on the wall
Noises down the hall
Life doesn't frighten me at all
Bad dogs barking loud
Big ghosts in a cloud
Life doesn't frighten me at all.

Mean old Mother Goose
Lions on the loose
They don't frighten me at all
Dragons breathing flame
On my counterpane
That doesn't frighten me at all.

I go boo
Make them shoo
I make fun
Way them run
I won't cry
So they fly
I just smile
They go wild
Life doesn't frighten me at all.

Tough guys in a fight
All alone at night
Life doesn't frighten me at all.
Panthers in the park
Strangers in the dark
No, they don't frighten me at all.

That new classroom where
Boys all pull my hair
(Kissy little girls
With their hair in curls)
They don't frighten me at all.

Don't show me frogs and snakes
And listen for my scream,
If I'm afraid at all
It's only in my dreams.

I've got a magic charm
That I keep up my sleeve,
I can walk the ocean floor
And never have to breathe.

Life doesn't frighten me at all
Not at all
Not at all
Life doesn't frighten me at all.

Maya Angelou

AFTERWORD

This letter is a sort of afterword because I think you're the kind of person who wants to read afterwords to books.

They are weird things, afterwords. You hope a bit that if you've done your job well enough you won't need to say anything more, and yet when I think about you closing this book, I feel like there's still more I want to say. I want to say something about this book, and about poems generally, and about where you might be going next.

Because although you've just finished this book, I want to talk to you about how this book is a beginning, a sort of guide book, or a map. You can think, "That poem was cool. I liked that", and then think, "I'd like to see more of that", and look it up. You can look up the author, or other poems that are the same kind of poem. You can look up other anthologies with the poem in, to see what poems other people think are like the poem you like.

Look, this book isn't the only anthology out there. (It's not even the only one by me.) All anthologies will have poems with something in common, and all anthologies will be different. This one is mine – full of poems almost all by women and girls that I love and want you to know. I hope these poems make you feel things. Some of them you'll love, and some of them you won't, and some of them I hope will stick with you in ways you don't even know yet. I hope they'll keep meaning things to you now, and future-you, and future-future-you.

The other week, I told someone about a poem I first read when I was maybe nine, and he read it out to me, and I heard in his voice that the poem was something new to him, and because it was new to him it started being new to me again, too. I've known that poem for twenty years and it was still just straight up surprising to me, how good it is, how rapidly it can change the rhythm of your heart. The poem was 'Tarantella', by Hilaire Belloc, which isn't in this book because Hilaire Belloc was a man; you should look it up. That's one of the things I mean, about this book being a beginning. There's so many poems out there that aren't in this book, and I hope the poems in this book sort of light your way to those poems, too.

I hope the poems in this book light your way to all sorts of things. Think of these poems not like still pictures, but more like doors: things you can push on, and that will open on to other things. This is a metaphor, but you get it. And they won't always mean the same things to you, poems, even these poems. You can read a poem, like, ninety-nine times, and then the hundredth time you go, "Oh", and it's different again. The door goes somewhere else. And sometimes it's just opening on to a feeling, and sometimes it opens on to another door, another poem. Another poem reminds you of a painting, which reminds you of another poem, and then another door opens. Baby, the world is full of doors. Find them. Open them. Keep opening them.

I hope you find poems I've never heard of.

I hope, generally, that you do things I've never heard of, and make things I've never seen before, and say things I've never even thought of in my life.

I hope you make anthologies that baffle me, with poets I don't recognise and poems I don't understand. I hope you make books you'd have to explain to me, patiently and kindly. This is the thing: I hope you outgrow this book, not because I haven't tried my best, but because as you grow up and read more and learn more and do more, I hope that your best is better than mine.

I'm writing this afterword in a summer when it seems that many things are on the cusp of change. The world is having big conversations about the kind of legacy we want to leave for your generation, and the kind of Earth we want you to inherit. Actually, we're really talking about the kind of Earth you have already inherited. We are going to make it better, I think. I hope.

We're talking about global warming and climate change, and what we can do to make things better for our planet. We're talking about our rights and responsibilities as children of the Earth, about what we have to do, to change things before it's too late.

We're talking about gender, and race, and class, by which I mean we're talking about how who you are and where you come from and how you look and speak and feel can change the ways people treat you, and whether that's fair.

We're talking about the ways life has been harder, historically, for women and girls, and how in some places and some situations it's still harder for women and girls. We're talking about all the ways there are of being a girl, and all the things that means. We're talking about the ways life continues to be harder for people who don't have white skin, the ways that racism is woven into lots of societies, and how difficult it is to start to unpick that terrible inequality. We're talking about how some people have a lot of money and some people have basically none, and how who gets the money is also often connected to whether you're a man, or whether you're white.

We're talking about how the world is set up for people who want to marry someone of the opposite gender (like, a man who wants to marry a woman, or the other way round) and how much harder it can be if you fall in love with someone who doesn't fit into that pattern. We're talking about how gender is maybe more complicated than most people used to think, and how much harder it can be if you don't fall into those patterns either. We're talking about why it's unfair, and who made it this way.

We're talking about how many ways there are to love, and how many ways there are to live, and how many ways there are to be, and how we can make life fair for all of us.

Now, listen, I know what you're thinking. You're thinking, "This is just a poetry book. Why do we need to talk about all of this in a poetry book?"

And the answer is this: because there's no such thing as "just". Nothing is "just"; everything has meaning, if we let it. We can find all sorts of meaning in everything we do, and everything we do gets to be part of the fight to change things.

And this is especially true when we think about art, and poetry is art. Art shows us what we have in common, no matter where we come from or who we are or who we love or what we look like. Art shows us what it is to be a person; it explains feelings and ideas you never knew there were words for, and it shows us that we're not alone. There's always someone who gets it, and I hope in this book you've found someone who gets it. Someone who gets you.

When we choose poetry to put in a book, we have to think, "What do I love about this poem? Who made this poem? Why this poem? Why not that poem? Who showed me this poem, and why?"

Mostly we think about "learning to read" as a thing that stops when we're really small – but this isn't true. We have to keep learning, all the time. In this book you've met poets from all over the world, of all ages and nationalities and skin colours. They're almost all women or girls (for all the reasons we talked about in the Introduction), and all of them have something to say: something new, something necessary, something important. I have learned so much from all of them. Every time I read the poems in this book – every time I remember one on the bus, or on the phone, or falling asleep – I learn something else. I get to think about the world the way someone else does, which makes me think about how I think about the world, and I get to think about the ways we're the same and the ways we're different. I have loved it.

And that is the reason I want to say to you: make your own collection, if you can. When you see a poem you love, write it down. Copy it out. Print it off. Take a screenshot. Take a photo. Whatever. Write it down; learn it by heart, even. Keep it with you. Tell someone about it.

I started this afterword to say something to you about where I thought you might be going next – about the world and how it's waiting for you – but the truth is, I don't know. I don't know where you're going, or what you're going to read and I don't know what you're going to do at all with this one wild and precious life of yours – and I am so excited to find out.

Love, always,

Ella
x

Ella Risbridger

INDEX OF POEMS

INDEX OF POETS

INDEX OF FIRST LINES

ACKNOWLEDGEMENTS

Bella Akhmadulina: 'Small Aircraft' from Fever and Other New Poems by Bella Akhmadulina. Copyright © 1969 by Geoffrey Dutton. Used by permission of HarperCollins Publishers. **Maya Angelou**: 'Life Doesn't Frighten Me' from And Still I Rise: A Book of Poems by Maya Angelou. Copyright © Maya Angelou 1978. Used by permission of Random House, an imprint and division of Penguin Random House LLC. All rights reserved. 'Life Doesn't Frighten Me' reprinted with permission of Little, Brown Book Group Limited. **Ruth Awolola**: 'On Forgetting That I Am a Tree' © Ruth Awolola from Rising Stars. Reproduced with permission of Otter-Barry Books. **Siana Bangura**: '3.05am' and 'Day One' by Siana Bangura. Copyright © Siana Bangura. Reproduced with permission of Siana Bangura. **Zeynep Beler**: 'Pink' by Zeynep Beler. Copyright © Z. Beler. Reproduced with permission of Z. Beler. **Valerie Bloom**: 'First Contact' © Valerie Bloom 2000 from Whoop an' Shout (Macmillan) and 'Why Is It?' © Valerie Bloom 2000 from Let Me Touch the Sky (Macmillan). Reprinted with permission of Eddison Pearson Ltd on behalf of Valerie Bloom. **Jean Binta Breeze**: 'Dreamer' by Jean Binta Breeze from Third World Girl: Selected Poems, with Live DVD (Bloodaxe Books, 2011). Reproduced with permission of Bloodaxe Books. **Victoria Adukwei Bulley**: 'Auntie Lucille' by Victoria Adukwei Bulley. Copyright © Victoria Adukwei Bulley. Reprinted with permission of Victoria Adukwei Bulley. **Anne Carson**: 'Fragment 104a' by Sappho, translated by Anne Carson, If Not, Winter: Fragments of Sappho by Anne Carson. Reproduced with permission of Little, Brown Book Group and '104A [Evening]' from If Not, Winter: Fragments of Sappho by Sappho, translated by Anne Carson © 2002 by Anne Carson. Used by permission of Alfred A. Knopf, an imprint of the Knopf Doubleday Publishing Group, a division of Penguin Random House LLC. All rights reserved. **Heather Christle**: 'People Are a Living Structure Like a Coral Reef' by Heather Christle from What Is Amazing © 2012 by Heather Christle. Published by Wesleyan University Press. Used with permission. **Lucille Clifton**: Excerpt from 'Admonitions' from The Collected Poems of Lucille Clifton. Copyright © 1969, 1987 by Lucille Clifton. Reprinted with the permission of The Permissions Company, LLC on behalf of BOA Editions Ltd. **Mandy Coe**: 'Cancan' by Mandy Coe © Mandy Coe. First appeared in Hot Heads, Warm Hearts, Cold Streets (Stanley Thornes). **Afua Cooper**: 'Kensington Market'. Copyright © Afua Cooper. Reproduced with permission of Afua Cooper. **Wendy Cope**: 'The Orange' by Wendy Cope (© Wendy Cope 1992) is printed by permission of United Agents on behalf of Wendy Cope. First published in Serious Concerns by Faber & Faber Ltd, reprinted with permission of Faber & Faber Ltd. **Yrsa Daley-Ward**: 'What is Now Will Soon be Past' from bone by Yrsa Daley-Ward. Copyright © 2014, 2017 by Yrsa Daley-Ward. Used by permission of Penguin Books, an imprint of Penguin Publishing Group, a division of Penguin Random House LLC. All rights reserved. From bone by Yrsa Daley-Ward published by Penguin. Copyright © Yrsa Daley-Ward 2014, 2017. Published by Penguin Books 2014, 2017. Reprinted by permission of Penguin Books Limited. **Beatrice Schenk de Regniers**: 'Keep a Poem in Your Pocket' by Beatrice Schenk de Regniers © Beatrice Schenk de Regniers. Reprinted with permission of the Estate of Beatrice Schenk de Regniers. **Jan Dean**: 'Rosa Parks' by Jan Dean from Reaching the Stars: Poems About Extraordinary Women and Girls, first published in 2017 by Pan Macmillan. Reproduced by permission of Macmillan Publishers International Limited. **Imtiaz Dharker**: 'How to Cut a Pomegranate' and 'Carving' by Imtiaz Dharker from The Terrorist at My Table (Bloodaxe Books, 2006). Reproduced with permission of Bloodaxe Books. **Berlie Doherty**: 'Ghost in the Garden' originally published in Walking on Air (Hodder Children's Books, 1999). Copyright © Berlie Doherty 1993. Reprinted with permission of David Higham Associates. **Carol Ann Duffy**: 'Mrs Hamilton's Register', 'Your Grandmother', 'Don't Be Scared', and 'Brave Enough' by Carol Ann Duffy. Copyright © Carol Ann Duffy. Reproduced by permission of the author c/o Rogers, Coleridge & White Ltd. **Eleanor Farjeon**: 'It was Long Ago' and 'Cats' by Eleanor Farjeon published in Blackbird Has Spoken by Macmillan. Reproduced with permission of David Higham Associates. **Hillary-Anne Farley**: 'This is a Poem' by Hillary-Anne Farley was originally published in Miracles: Poems by Children of the English-Speaking World, edited by Richard Lewis and published by Simon & Schuster, New York, 1966. Copyright © 1966 by Richard Lewis. **Denice Frohman**: 'A Woman's Place' by Denice Frohman. Copyright © Denice Frohman. Reproduced with permission of Denice Frohman. **Elaine Gallagher**: 'Tipsy' and 'Questions' (Extract). Copyright © Elaine Gallagher 2014. Reproduced with permission of Elaine Gallagher. **Nikita Gill**: '93 Percent Stardust' by Nikita Gill © Nikita Gill. Reproduced with permission of David Higham Associates. **Nikki Giovanni**: 'Winter Poem' from The Collected Poetry of Nikki Giovanni. Copyright © 2003 by Nikki Giovanni. Used by permission of HarperCollins Publishers. **Salena Godden**: 'Soup' by Salena Godden. Copyright © Salena Godden 2021. Reproduced with permission of Salena Godden. **Amanda Gorman**: 'The Hill We Climb' Copyright © 2021 by Amanda Gorman. Reprinted by permission of the author. **Eloise Greenfield**: 'Honey, I Love' and 'Harriet Tubman' from Honey, I Love and Other Love Poems by Eloise Greenfield. Used by permission of HarperCollins Publishers. Text of 'Honey, I Love' and 'Harriet Tubman' from Honey, I Love. Copyright © Eloise Greenfield 1978. Used by permission of Scott Treimel, NY. **Nikki Grimes**: 'Journey's End' © Nikki Grimes 2021 from Legacy: Women Poets of the Harlem Renaissance, Bloomsbury Publishing Inc. **Triska Hamid**: 'This Ray' by Triska Hamid. Copyright © Triska Hamid. Reproduced with permission of Triska Hamid. **Joy Harjo**: 'Remember' by Joy Harjo. Copyright © 1983 by Joy Harjo from She Had Some Horses by Joy Harjo. Used by permission of W. W. Norton & Company, Inc. **Phoebe Hesketh**: 'Sally' from The Leave Train, Enitharmon, 1994. Copyright © Phoebe Hesketh 1994. Reprinted with permission of the literary executors of Phoebe Hesketh. **Elisabeth Hewer**: 'Sometimes, Change is One Girl', 'Here are Girls Like Lions', and 'You're Still Going' by Elisabeth Hewer. Copyright © Elisabeth Hewer. All reproduced with permission of Elisabeth Hewer. **Selima Hill**: 'Soup' by Selima Hill from Gloria: Selected Poems (Bloodaxe Books, 2008). **Jackie Hosking**: 'Wherever' by Jackie Hosking © Jackie Hosking. Reproduced with permission of Jackie Hosking. **Kirsten Irving**: 'From Boudicca, Queen of the Iceni, to Gaius Suetonius Paullinus, on the Occasion of his Invasion' first appeared in The Head That Wears a Crown: Poems about Kings and Queens (The Emma Press, 2018) © Kirsten Irving. **Elizabeth Jennings**: 'Fragment for the Dark' by Elizabeth Jennings from The Collected Poems by Elizabeth Jennings published by Carcanet Press. Reproduced with permission of David Higham Associates Limited. **Jenny Joseph**: 'In a Dark Stone' © Jenny Joseph. Copyright © The Estate of Jenny Joseph. First published in Ghosts and Other Company, Bloodaxe Books, 1995. Reproduced with permission of Johnson & Alcock Ltd. **Jackie Kay**: 'Grandpa's Soup' from The Frog Who Dreamed She Was an Opera Singer by Jackie Kay. Copyright © Jackie Kay 1998. Used by permission of The Wylie Agency (UK) Limited. 'An Old Woman's Fire' by Jackie Kay © Jackie Kay 2007 from Red, Cherry, Red, Bloomsbury Publishing PLC. 'Brendon Gallacher' from Darling: New & Selected Poems (Bloodaxe Books, 2007). Reproduced with permission of Bloodaxe Books. **Amineh Abou Kerech**: 'To Make a Homeland' by Amineh Abou Kerech. Copyright © Amineh Abou Kerech. Reproduced with permission of Amineh Abou Kerech. **Helen Lamb**: 'Spell of the Bridge' by Helen Lamb. Copyright © The Estate of Helen Lamb. Reproduced with permission of the Estate of Helen Lamb. **Lois Lenski**: 'Sing A Song of People' by Lois Lenski. Copyright © Lois Lenski. Reprinted by permission of SLL/Sterling Lord Literistic, Inc. **Ada Limón**: 'How to Triumph Like a Girl' from Bright Dead Things. Copyright © Ada Limón 2015. Reprinted with the permission of The Permissions Company, LLC on behalf of Milkweed Editions. **Liz Lochhead**: 'Nina's Song' © Liz Lochhead, published by Birlinn Limited in Fugitive Colours. Reproduced with permission of the Birlinn Limited through PLSclear. **Eve Merriam**: 'How to Eat a Poem'. Copyright © 1971 by Eve Merriam. Originally published by Antheneum Books. Currently published in It Doesn't Always Have to Rhyme: A Book of Poetry. Reprinted by permission of Curtis Brown, Ltd. **Marianne Moore**: 'I May, I Might, I Must' by Marianne Moore from the New Collected Poems of Marianne Moore by Marianne Moore, published by Faber & Faber Ltd. Copyright © 1959 by Marianne Moore. Copyright renewed © 1987 by Lawrence E. Brinn and Louise Crane, executors of the Estate of Marianne Moore. From The Complete Poems of Marianne Moore by Marianne Moore. Used by permission of Viking Books, an imprint of Penguin Publishing Group, a division of Penguin Random House LLC. All rights reserved. **Pamela Mordecai**: 'Lament of an Arawak Child'. Copyright © Pamela Mordecai. Reproduced with permission of Pamela Mordecai. **Michaela Morgan**: 'Malala' by Michaela Morgan from Reaching the Stars: Poems About Extraordinary Women and Girls, first published in 2017 by Pan Macmillan. Reproduced by permission of Macmillan Publishers International Limited. **Marilyn Nelson**: 'Moonlily' by Marilyn Nelson © Marilyn Nelson. Reprinted with permission of Blue Flower Arts LLC. **Judith Nicholls**: 'Dog' © Judith Nicholls 1987 from Midnight Forest by Judith Nicholls, published by Faber & Faber. Reprinted by permission of the author. 'Starfish' and 'Breakfast for One' © Judith Nicholls 2020. Reprinted by permission of the author. **Grace Nichols**: 'Sea Timeless Song' by Grace Nichols from The Fat Black Woman's Poems © Grace Nichols. Reproduced with permission of Little, Brown Book Group Limited. 'Granny Granny Please Comb My Hair' and 'I Like to Stay Up' from Come on Into My Tropical Garden. Copyright © Grace Nichols 1988. Reproduced with permission of Curtis Brown Group Ltd on behalf of Grace Nichols. 'Mistress Cooper' and 'Tabby'. Copyright © Grace Nichols 2000. Reproduced with permission of Curtis Brown Group Ltd on behalf of Grace Nichols. 'Seven Sisters' from Picasso, I Want My Face Back. Copyright © Grace Nichols 2009. Reproduced with permission of Curtis Brown Group Ltd on behalf of Grace Nichols. **Julie O'Callaghan**: 'Sister in a Whale' by Julie O'Callaghan from Tell Me This Is Normal: New & Selected Poems (Bloodaxe Books, 2008). Reproduced with permission of Bloodaxe Books. **Mary Oliver**: 'The Summer Day' from House of Light by Mary Oliver, published by Beacon Press, Boston. Copyright © Mary Oliver 1990. Used herewith by permission of the Charlotte Sheedy Literary Agency, Inc. **Linda Pastan**: 'A New Poet' and 'Blizzard' from Carnival Evening: New and Selected Poems (1968-1998) by Linda Pastan. Copyright © 1998 by Linda Pastan. Used by permission of W. W. Norton & Company, Inc. **Rachel Piercey**: 'Bath Time' by Rachel Piercey © Rachel Piercey 2014. First published in Best Friends Forever (The Emma Press, 2014). **Rachel Plummer**: 'Selkie' by Rachel Plummer © Rachel Plummer 2019. Reprinted with the kind permission of The Emma Press. **Shazea Quraishi**: 'Ghazal with Rain and Birds' by Shazea Quraishi. Copyright © Shazea Quraishi. Reproduced with permission of Shazea Quraishi. **Laura Ranger**: 'God' by Laura Ranger. Copyright © Laura Ranger. Reproduced with permission of Laura Ranger. **Vita Sackville-West**: 'Full Moon' by Vita Sackville-West. Reproduced with permission of Curtis Brown Group Ltd, London on behalf of the Estate of Vita Sackville-West. Copyright © Vita Sackville-West 1922. **Olive Senior**: 'The Birth of Islands' by Olive Senior. Copyright © Olive Senior 2005. Published in Over the Roofs of the World, Toronto: Insomniac Press, 2005. Reproduced with permission of Olive Senior. **Stevie Smith**: 'In My Dreams' by Stevie Smith from Collected Poems of Stevie Smith. Copyright © 1972 by Stevie Smith. Reprinted by permission of New Directions Publishing Corp. Collected Poems of Stevie Smith published by Faber & Faber and reprinted with permission of Faber & Faber Ltd. **May Swenson**: 'The Centaur' by May Swenson. Copyright © 1958, 2013 May Swenson. Used with permission of The Literary Estate of May Swenson. All rights reserved. **Kai Cheng Thom**: 'There is a Poem' by Kai Cheng Thom. Copyright © Kai Cheng Thom 2017. Reprinted with permission of Arsenal Pulp Press. **Kate Wakeling**: 'Comet' by Kate Wakeling. Copyright © Kate Wakeling. Reproduced with permission of The Emma Press. **Alice Walker**: 'Lodestar' by Alice Walker from Taking the Arrow Out of the Heart by Alice Walker. Copyright © 2018 by Alice Walker. Reprinted by permission of 37 Ink, a Division of Simon & Schuster, Inc. 'Lodestar' by Alice Walker from Taking the Arrow Out of the Heart published by Simon & Schuster and reprinted with permission of David Higham Associates. **Janet S. Wong**: 'A Suitcase of Seaweed' by Janet S. Wong. Copyright © 1996 by Janet S. Wong. **Elli Woollard**: 'Like a Sun' by Elli Woollard © Elli Woollard. Reproduced with permission of the author.

Every effort has been made to obtain permission to reproduce copyright material, but there may have been cases where we have been unable to establish contact with a copyright holder. The publisher would be happy to correct any omissions in future printings.